THE 5 LOVE LANGUAGES®

OF TEENAGERS

WORKBOOK

THE 5 LOVE LANGUAGES® OF TEENAGERS

#1 *NEW YORK TIMES* BESTSELLER

Gary Chapman

WORKBOOK

NORTHFIELD PUBLISHING

CHICAGO

Developed with the assistance of Peachtree Publishing Services (www.peachtreeeditorial.com). Special thanks to Randy Southern.
Interior design: Erik M. Peterson
Cover design: Faceout Studio
Cover image of bokeh copyright © 2023 by Ole moda/Shutterstock (1469341238). All rights reserved.

ISBN: 978-0-8024-3297-1

We hope you enjoy this book from Northfield Publishing. Our goal is to provide high-quality, thought-provoking books and products that connect truth to your real needs and challenges. For more information on other books and products that will help you with all your important relationships, go to northfieldpublishing.com or write to:

Northfield Publishing
820 N. LaSalle Boulevard
Chicago, IL 60610

1 3 5 7 9 10 8 6 4 2

Printed in the United States of America

CONTENTS

INTRODUCTION

WELCOME to a labor of love.

The thirteen lessons in this book were created for one purpose: to strengthen and deepen your loving relationship with your teenagers. The process won't be easy. Nothing worthwhile ever is. This study will pose some challenging questions. It will take you outside your comfort zone. It will even require you to do homework.

But this isn't busywork. These lessons give you workable strategies for applying the principles of *The 5 Love Languages of Teenagers.* They offer glimpses of your parenting potential when you speak your teenager's love language.

If you're working through this study alone, take heart. Your solo efforts will likely have a profound impact on your relationship with your teen. Throughout *The 5 Love Languages of Teenagers,* you'll find accounts of difficult parenting challenges that were overcome by one parent's commitment to learning his or her teenager's love language.

If you're working through this study as a couple, let patience, grace, and humor be your companions. Learning a new love language can be difficult, and there's more than a little trial and error involved. Show your appreciation for your spouse's efforts to communicate love in ways that are meaningful to your teenager, no matter how clumsy those efforts are at first. And be sure to celebrate when those efforts hit the mark.

If you're working through this study in a group, pay attention to what your fellow group members share. Inspiration and wisdom can be found in unexpected places. In your interactions with fellow group members, be generous with your encouragement and sparing with your criticism. Ask appropriate follow-up questions to show your interest in their success. See *The 5 Love Languages of Teenagers* Leader's Guide on pages 112–13 for helpful suggestions in facilitating group discussions.

Regardless of how you approach this study, you should be aware that the lessons in this book will require a significant investment of time and effort. There's a lot of important material in these pages. But it's virtually a risk-free investment. You will see dividends. And the more of yourself you pour into this workbook, the greater your dividends will be.

Enjoy the journey!

GARY CHAPMAN

OBJECTIVE

In reading this chapter, you will learn how the search for independence and identity among today's teenagers is similar to and different from that of past generations of teenagers—and how to show empathy, support, and love to your teenager throughout the search.

UNDERSTANDING TODAY'S TEENAGERS

INSTRUCTIONS: Complete this first lesson after reading chapter 1 ("Understanding Today's Teenagers," pp. 15–27) of *The 5 Love Languages of Teenagers*.

KEY TERMS

Independence: one of the two underlying themes of teenage culture, it involves becoming a self-governing person by taking on responsibility, making decisions by yourself, and charting a course for adulthood.

Identity: one of the two underlying themes of teenage culture, it involves figuring out who you are, establishing a unique persona, and shaping your perception of where you belong.

OPENING QUESTIONS

1. What were you like as a teenager? What would your parents say you were like as a teenager? What would your friends say you were like as a teenager? What would your teachers, instructors, or coaches say you were like as a teenager? What would your rivals, competitors, or nemeses say you were like as a teenager?

2. If you could choose certain experiences from your teenage years for your child to experience, what would they be? Why? If you could spare your child from experiencing certain things from your teenage years, what would they be? Why?

THINK ABOUT IT

3. Dr. Chapman writes, **"The places where the teenager expresses independence and identity have changed through the years, but the means continue to be basically the same."** What are some of those means? Regarding teenage tastes, what does Dr. Chapman say you can be certain of?

4. **"Accepting and adapting to the changes that take place in the teen's body"** is one challenge that virtually all young people face. What questions do these physiological changes spur in the mind of a teenager? In addition to experiencing physical changes, teenagers also learn to reason and think logically. Why is it important for parents to recognize these new mental capabilities?

5. Teenagers also examine the belief systems with which they were raised to determine **"if those beliefs are worthy of [their] commitment."** How do wise parents react to their teen's questioning? How do those same wise parents address their teenager's emerging sexuality? How do they address their teen's questions about the future?

6. As Dr. Chapman points out, **"The contemporary teenager is exposed to far more cultural stimuli than his parents ever could have dreamed at his age."** Give some examples from your own experience. What cultural stimuli does your teenager face that you never had to?

7. Dr. Chapman writes, **"A . . . cultural factor that influences the contemporary teenager is the fragmented nature of the modern American family."** What statistics does he use to support his claim? What types of fragmentation have sociologists observed?

8. How is today's overtly sexual atmosphere different from the atmosphere of past generations of teenagers who rebelled against their parents' sexual mores? What does a **"truly post-Christian"** world of neutral moral and religious views look like?

9. Dr. Chapman reminds us that, amid these sobering realities, there is good news: **"Contemporary teenagers are looking to parents for guidance."** In what areas do parents have especially strong influence? How can you maximize your influence in your teenager's life?

TAKE IT HOME

The first chapter highlighted some of the general trends of current and past generations of teenagers. Now it's time to think in terms of specifics. Fill in the chart below, comparing your experience as a teen with your child's experience as a teen.

	YOU	YOUR TEEN
Assets		
Challenges		
Goals		
Mistakes		
Passions		

FINDING COMMON GROUND WITH YOUR TEEN

The two circles represent you and your teenager. Fill in the diagram using information from the chart you completed on the previous page. For example, if social media is a much bigger challenge for your teen than it was for you, write "Social Media" in the part of your teen's circle that's unique to them. Likewise, if you and your teen are both ambitious, write "Ambition" in the area where your circles overlap.

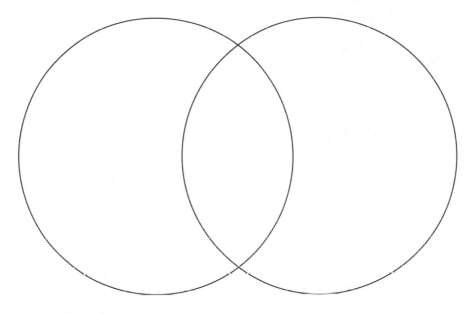

How can you use those areas of overlap to strengthen your rapport with your teenager and help him or her see you as someone who can empathize?

How can you address the experiences of your teenager that are far outside your area of overlap? How can you build trust with your teen so that he or she feels comfortable helping you understand those experiences?

LOVE CHALLENGE

To understand the challenges your teenager will encounter, you may need to step out of your comfort zone and confront some of the realities that your son or daughter faces. What will you do this week to get a better understanding of your teenager's world?

Use this space for more notes, quotes, or lessons learned from the chapter.

OBJECTIVE

In reading this chapter, you will learn how unconditional love lays
the groundwork for a healthy, fulfilling parent-teen relationship.

THE KEY: LOVE FROM PARENTS

INSTRUCTIONS: Complete this second lesson after reading chapter 2 ("The Key: Love from Parents," pp. 29–41) of *The 5 Love Languages of Teenagers.*

KEY TERMS

Emotional love: a soul-deep feeling of connection, acceptance, and nurturing that a teenager receives from his or her parents in an emotionally healthy family dynamic.

Primary love language: the love language that most profoundly impacts a person and causes him or her to feel loved.

Love tank: the emotional reservoir inside everyone that is filled when people speak to us in our primary love language.

Emotional intelligence: the ability to read emotions in others, to communicate effectively in the nonverbal realm, to handle the ups and downs of daily life, and to have appropriate expectations for relationships.

OPENING QUESTIONS

1. What were your parents' favorite ways to express their love for you? Why do you think they preferred those specific methods? How did you respond to their expressions of love?

2. If you could have changed anything about the way your parents expressed their love for you, what would it be? Why?

THINK ABOUT IT

3. News reports of teen violence, teen mental health struggles, teen addictions, and other teen crises can be distressing for parents. But Dr. Chapman points out, **"The reality is that most of what we read in the newspaper and hear via the media deals with the 10 percent of troubled teenagers."** What is the key for teenagers to effectively navigate dangerous cultural waters and have the confidence to face negative influences?

4. Dr. Chapman points out that if emotional bonding between parent and child doesn't take place, **"the child's emotional development will be plagued with feelings of insecurity."** What is the prerequisite for bonding?

5. **"Emotional connectedness requires communication."** Why does Dr. Chapman say that **"the meal table is one of the best places to build emotional connectedness with teenagers"**? What guideline does he suggest for family mealtimes?

6. Describe what happens in the thought processes of a child who feels accepted by his or her parents. Describe what happens to a child who feels rejected by his or her parents. How can you make your teenager feel genuinely accepted?

7. Dr. Chapman quotes Bob, a father of two teenagers, who worried that showing acceptance to a misbehaving teen would send the wrong signal. What theological illustration does Dr. Chapman offer to clarify the goal of acceptance? What does unconditional love say to a child?

8. What does it mean to nurture your teenager? Why is it important for parents to nurture themselves first? Why are a positive attitude and a caring spirit essential assets for nurturing parents?

9. What happens when a teenager's love tank is empty? In contrast, what happens when a teenager receives significant amounts of emotional love?

TAKE IT HOME

There are different ways to show emotional love to your teenager. Some are more effective than others, depending on your teen's emotional makeup. Let's take a closer look at them. How often do you use the following methods for showing love to your teenager?

Offering sincere compliments, encouragement, affirmation, support, and other verbal expressions of affection

Rarely   Frequently

Why do you use this method as frequently or as infrequently as you do?

Giving hugs, high fives, shoulder massages, and other forms of appropriate, affectionate physical contact

Rarely   Frequently

Why do you use this method as frequently or as infrequently as you do?

Spending focused, uninterrupted, one-on-one time together, doing things they enjoy

Rarely   Frequently

Why do you use this method as frequently or as infrequently as you do?

Performing meaningful acts, such as painting your teen's bedroom or making their favorite snack after a hard day

Rarely   Frequently

Why do you use this method as frequently or as infrequently as you do?

Giving thoughtful, well-chosen gifts

Rarely   Frequently

Why do you use this method as frequently or as infrequently as you do?

LEARNING WHAT WORKS

Think of the last time you expressed your love for your teenager in a way that really seemed to resonate with him or her. What were the circumstances?

What specifically did you do?

How did your teenager react?

How do you explain your teen's reaction?

What did you take away from the experience?

LOVE CHALLENGE

Dr. Chapman emphasizes, **"To nurture your teenager first requires that you nurture yourself."** All of us have emotional weaknesses that we need to address, whether it's anger issues or a negative attitude. What steps will you take this week to address an emotional weakness in yourself so that you can better nurture your teenager?

Use this space for more notes, quotes, or lessons learned from the chapter.

OBJECTIVE

In reading this chapter, you will learn how to use words of affirmation
to express love in ways that fill your teenager's emotional love tank.

LOVE LANGUAGE #1: WORDS OF AFFIRMATION

INSTRUCTIONS: Complete this third lesson after reading chapter 3 ("Love Language #1: Words of Affirmation," pp. 43–62) of *The 5 Love Languages of Teenagers*.

KEY TERM

Words of affirmation: verbal and written expressions of love, appreciation, and encouragement that communicate love in profound ways for teenagers who speak that love language.

OPENING QUESTIONS

1. What's the highest compliment someone could give you or the most impactful thing someone could say to you? Why would those words be especially meaningful to you? What impact would they have on you?

2. Describe a time when you said something that impacted another person—either positively or negatively. What were the circumstances? What did you say? What impact did your words have? What did you take away from the experience?

THINK ABOUT IT

3. Dr. Chapman begins the chapter with the story of Brad, a teenager whose parents asked him to talk to Dr. Chapman. If your teenager were in Dr. Chapman's office, what would your son or daughter say about your parent-child communication? If your teen's primary love language was words of affirmation, how do you think he or she would describe the condition of his or her love tank right now? Explain.

4. Dr. Chapman writes, **"All of us have an emotional love tank and when that love tank is full—when we really feel loved by the important people in our lives—the world looks bright and we can discuss our differences in a positive way."** What happens when the love tank is empty?

5. What is the **"melody playing in the mind of a teenager"**? What must that melody be harmonized with? What happens when **"parents do not account for this new song that is being played in the teenager's mind"**?

6. Dr. Chapman says, **"If there is a stage of life where humans need more affirming words, it would certainly be the teenage years."** What circumstances do teenagers face that make affirming words so necessary?

7. What two factors are important in giving words of praise to teenagers? Why is flattery ineffective on teenagers? What happens when parents try to use it? Why are sweeping general statements of praise ineffective? What can parents do if they aren't able to praise the results of their teenager's efforts?

8. What is the most common statement of verbal affection? What happens when teenagers don't hear those words from their parents? Why do some parents—fathers especially—have trouble speaking those words? How can they work through those difficulties? How can you use statements of verbal affection to focus on your teenager's attributes or personality?

9. According to Dr. Chapman, when do words of affirmation **"often speak louder"**? What would those scenarios look like in your family? Who are the best candidates to help you express your love for your teenager through words of affection?

TAKE IT HOME

Conduct a casual interview with your teen to get a sense of the words of affirmation that are most meaningful to him or her. Use the following questions as needed and add some of your own if possible. Tailor the questions to fit your teen's personality and circumstances.

What's the best thing a teacher or coach ever said—or could ever say—to you?

What's the best thing a friend ever said—or could ever say—to you?

What's the best thing a family member ever said—or could ever say—to you?

What's the best thing a stranger ever said—or could ever say—to you?

PERSONALIZED MESSAGES

For each of the following scenarios, list some words of affirmation that you think would be meaningful to your teenager.

A sticky note left on the bathroom mirror for your teen to see first thing in the morning

While saying goodbye as you head off to work or your teen heads off to school

A note hidden in your teen's lunch

A random text in the middle of the day

When your teen is feeling anxious about a test

After your teen plays a great game or gives an impressive performance

After your teen has a rough game or performance

In a conversation with others that you want your teen to hear—or hear about

When your teen is facing a major life decision

When you say goodnight to your teen

LOVE CHALLENGE

Dr. Chapman recommends keeping a notebook in which you write statements you can use to affirm, praise, and encourage your teenager. What will be the first statements you write in your notebook this week? For what circumstances or events in your teen's life should you prepare words of affirmation?

Use this space for more notes, quotes, or lessons learned from the chapter.

OBJECTIVE

In reading this chapter, you will learn how the purposeful use
of physical touch can fill your teenager's emotional love tank.

LOVE LANGUAGE #2: PHYSICAL TOUCH

INSTRUCTIONS: Complete this fourth lesson after reading chapter 4 ("Love Language #2: Physical Touch," pp. 65–82) of *The 5 Love Languages of Teenagers.*

KEY TERM

Physical touch: a love language in which a teenager experiences emotional wholeness through human contact.

OPENING QUESTIONS

1. In terms of healthy expressions of love through physical touch, how did your relationship with your parents change when you became a teenager? Which types of physical touch annoyed you as a teenager? Which types were acceptable? Why do you think you felt that way?

2. How did your parents react to your changing preferences? Did they honor your requests, or did they continue to treat you as a child in the way they used physical touch? How did their use of physical touch affect your relationship with them when you were a teenager?

THINK ABOUT IT

3. Dr. Chapman emphasizes, **"Teenagers are different from children. You cannot continue to give the same kind of touches in the same environments and in the same manner that you gave when they were younger."** What questions should parents ask before they try to speak the love language of physical touch?

4. Dr. Chapman encourages parents to **"learn the art of appropriate timing"** when it comes to physical touch with their teenagers. What two factors make that a difficult task? How do wise parents overcome that difficulty?

5. How does Dr. Chapman's contrast of the ten-year-old football player and the sixteen-year-old football player illustrate the importance of considering the appropriate place to speak the love language of physical touch to your teenager?

6. Dr. Chapman emphasizes the importance of being flexible when it comes to speaking the love language of physical touch. What is the key question that parents must ask? What factors complicate parents' attempts to show love through physical touch?

7. **"The good news about the love language of physical touch is that it can be easily spoken even when your teen's behavior is not pleasing."** How can you express your displeasure with your teen's behavior at the same time you're expressing love by physical touch?

8. Dr. Chapman points out that there's a tendency on the part of fathers to withdraw physical touch when their daughters approach puberty. Why is that a serious mistake?

9. Dr. Chapman concludes the chapter with testimonials from Victoria, Joel, Meredith, Barrett, and Jessica. What would you like to hear your teenager say about the way you show love and affection through physical touch?

TAKE IT HOME

If your teenager's primary love language is physical touch, how full is his or her love tank? How much purposeful physical touch does your teen receive from you in an average day? It's probably not something you've kept track of—before now. But it's something you need to know.

Let's start with a rough estimate, using yesterday as an example. Try to recall every interaction you had with your teen yesterday. How many times did you purposefully use physical touch—whether it was hugs, high fives, headlocks, or something else—to express love and affection to your teen?

Now let's check your math. Starting at the moment you wake up tomorrow, keep track of the number of times you express love to your teen through physical touch. Treat it like an average day. Don't go out of your way to pad your number. Your goal is to get a sense of what your teen experiences on a typical day. What number did you get? How did that compare with your estimate for yesterday? In other words, how accurate is your sense of how often you use physical touch with your teen?

What do these numbers tell you about your use of the physical touch love language in your relationship with your teen?

FIND OUT WHAT WORKS

Here are a few types of physical touch to try with your teenager. Keep track of your teen's reaction so that you know which types of touch to use in the future.

TOUCH CHALLENGE	YOUR TEEN'S REACTION
Create a unique handshake or hug routine with your teen, one you only use with each other.	
Give your teen a hug every time he or she leaves the house.	
Gently bump into your teen when you walk past each other.	
Playfully wrestle with your teen.	
Incorporate high fives and fist bumps into your daily interactions with your teen.	

LOVE CHALLENGE

The challenge that parents of a teenager face is figuring out what types of physical touch their teen is comfortable with—and then learning how to use those touches in purposeful and meaningful ways that fill the teen's emotional love tank. How will you rise to that challenge this week? What will you do to signal to your teen that you're serious about learning to speak the love language of physical touch?

Use this space for more notes, quotes, or lessons learned from the chapter.

In reading this chapter, you will learn how to use quality time, quality conversation, and quality activities to express love in ways that fill your teenager's emotional love tank.

LOVE LANGUAGE #3: QUALITY TIME

INSTRUCTIONS: Complete this fifth lesson after reading chapter 5 ("Love Language #3: Quality Time," pp. 85–108) of *The 5 Love Languages of Teenagers*.

KEY TERMS

Quality time: a way of expressing love through spending purposeful time with, and directing your full attention to, another person.

Quality conversation: empathetic dialogue in which two people share their experiences, thoughts, feelings, and desires in a friendly, uninterrupted context.

OPENING QUESTIONS

1. On an average day, how much time do you spend with your teenager? What would a breakdown of that time spent together look like? For example, how much time do you spend together during meals? While watching a show together? While traveling in the car?

2. How much of the time you spend with your teenager would you consider to be "quality time"? How do you define quality time? How much of the time you spend together would your teen consider to be quality time? How do you think your teen would define quality time?

THINK ABOUT IT

3. Dr. Chapman writes, **"Unfortunately the love language of quality time is much more difficult to speak than either words of affirmation or physical touch."** What is the key challenge parents face when it comes to quality time? According to Dr. Campbell, what happens to a teenager who doesn't receive focused attention?

4. What is the difference between proximity and togetherness? Using the illustration of a father and son watching a baseball game together, explain how a teenager might have two radically different reactions, depending on how that time together plays out.

5. What's the difference between the love language of words of affirmation and the quality conversation that's part of the love language of quality time? What does quality conversation sound like when you remember your teen's emerging independence and self-identity?

6. According to Dr. Chapman, **"Effective talking focuses on sharing your own thoughts, feelings, and desires, not on attacking those of the teenager."** What does he recommend as the simplest way to learn this approach? What's the difference between "you" statements and "I" statements? What's the difference between teaching and preaching?

7. Dr. Chapman points out, **"Teenagers are creatures of action. Many parents' most quality conversations will take place in association with some activity."** What activities are part of your teen's normal flow of life? What does it say to your teenager when you attend his or her activities? What impact does your presence have on your teen's development?

8. Dr. Chapman reminds parents that they **"may also learn to create environments for quality time with teenagers by planning and executing events outside the normal weekly routines."** Dr. Chapman explains how he piggybacked on his son's interest in Buddy Holly to plan a quality time excursion for the two of them. What would a similar gesture look like in your relationship with your teenager?

9. **"One common complaint among parents is that when their child becomes a teenager, they stop talking."** How does Dr. Chapman explain this change? What should parents do in that situation? How can they help open the door of communication?

TAKE IT HOME

Your first step in spending quality time with your teenager is finding the time to spend. On the planner page below, write out a typical daily schedule for yourself, from the time you wake up to the time you go to bed.

In the space below, write some specific ideas for adjusting your daily schedule to open up more time to spend with your teen. In some cases, it might mean cutting back in some area (say, screen time) and using the time saved to devote to your teen—perhaps in the form of a hobby or bike ride. In other cases, it might mean finding ways to include your teen in certain activities. For example, you might start exercising or cooking meals together. With a little creativity and sacrifice, you can find a surprising number of ways to spend more quality time with your teenager.

DAILY PLANNER
SCHEDULE

6:00 AM

7:00 AM

8:00 AM

9:00 AM

10:00 AM

11:00 AM

12:00 PM

1:00 PM

2:00 PM

3:00 PM

4:00 PM

5:00 PM

6:00 PM

7:00 PM

8:00 PM

9:00 PM

TURNING TIME TOGETHER INTO QUALITY TIME

Dr. Chapman points out that time spent with your teenager is not necessarily quality time. By the same token, any time you and your teen are together, even if it's just half an hour or so, can be quality time if you approach it as such. For each of the following scenarios, jot down a few ideas for making it quality time with your teen.

You and your teen attend your younger child's soccer game together.

You have thirty minutes to kill before church.

The rest of the family has plans, so it's just you and your teen for dinner.

Inclement weather closes your teen's school for the day.

LOVE CHALLENGE

Tomorrow you will have twenty-four hours to spend. What special gesture can you make in those twenty-four hours to signal to your teenager that you want to prioritize quality time with him or her?

Use this space for more notes, quotes, or lessons learned from the chapter.

OBJECTIVE

In reading this chapter, you will learn how to perform tasks and complete projects in ways that fill your teenager's emotional love tank.

LOVE LANGUAGE #4: ACTS OF SERVICE

INSTRUCTIONS: Complete this sixth lesson after reading chapter 6 ("Love Language #4: Acts of Service," pp. 111–125) of *The 5 Love Languages of Teenagers*.

KEY TERM

Acts of service: a love language in which a person experiences emotional wholeness when chores or tasks are done for his or her benefit.

OPENING QUESTIONS

1. What's the nicest thing anyone has ever done for you? What were the circumstances? Why was the gesture so meaningful to you? What did you appreciate most about it?

2. Which household chores is your teenager responsible for? How does your teen's workload compare with that of the rest of your family? How does your teen view his or her household workload? What is his or her least favorite chore? What would it mean to your teen if you occasionally completed that task yourself?

THINK ABOUT IT

3. Dr. Chapman reminds parents that the enormous amount of hard work we do **"takes on a dimension of nobility when you understand that such acts are powerful expressions of emotional love to your teenager."** What keeps parents from recognizing the full potential of their hard work?

4. Dr. Chapman points out, **"Loving service is not slavery."** What are the differences between the two?

5. Give an example of using acts of service as a means of manipulating your teen. Why does Dr. Chapman say **"manipulation is never an expression of love"**?

6. What are the two main desires of conscientious parents of teenagers? Why must parents choose their acts of service wisely? What is a good rule of thumb when it comes to acts of service?

7. Dr. Chapman says, **"I think it is helpful for parents to verbally explain to teenagers what they are doing."** Give an example of an explanation you would give your teenager regarding an act of service.

8. How can the right acts of service enhance your teenager's sense of identity? How can the right acts of service give your teenager a greater sense of independence?

9. Gray, Krystal, Todd, and Kristin spoke convincingly about the impact parental acts of service can have on teenagers. What would you like your teen to say about you?

TAKE IT HOME

Dr. Chapman writes, **"Parenting is a service-oriented vocation."** He suggests that if you really want to feel good about yourself as a parent, take a few minutes to calculate the number of things you've done for your child over the years. Here's a chance to do that. Come up with an estimate for each of the following categories.

Number of times you changed a diaper   _____

Number of times you did your child's laundry   _____

Number of times you served as your child's chauffeur   _____

Number of times you prepared and packed your
child's lunch for school   _____

Number of times you hosted parties, playdates, and sleepovers   _____

Number of times you bathed your child   _____

Number of times you read to your child   _____

Number of times you cooked meals for your child   _____

Number of times you cared for your child when
he or she was sick   _____

Number of times you fixed something for your child   _____

It's likely that neither you nor your child ever considered these things as acts of service. But you can change that—at least when it comes to the things you still do for your teenager. All you need to do is add a purposeful, personalized twist to the act—something that makes it feel special for your teen.

Choose three of the tasks above and write down a way you can turn each one into an act of service. For example, if you still pack your teen's lunch, you could add his or her favorite dessert occasionally.

HOW MUCH WOULD IT MEAN?

Below you'll find a list of acts of service. Rate each one on a scale of one to ten, based on how meaningful you think it would be to your teenager (with one being "not meaningful at all" and ten being "extremely meaningful"). We've left two slots blank for you to fill in with ideas that are specific to your family. After you've rated them all, talk to your teen about them. Get his or her reaction. Compare your numbers and talk about areas where there are notable discrepancies.

ACT OF SERVICE	YOU	TEEN
Choosing paint colors for your teen's room and painting it together		
Preparing study aids to help your teen study for a big test		
Dropping whatever you're doing to deliver a uniform that your teen forgot		
Taking your teen to his or her favorite restaurant to celebrate his or her birthday		
Doing your teen's least favorite household chore when he or she is busy		
Teaching your teen how to fix a flat tire		
Providing special care for your teen when he or she is sick		
Waking up early to make a surprise breakfast for your teen		
Volunteering for a community project together		
Washing your teen's car		
Making your teen's lunch before school		

LOVE CHALLENGE

Is there something that you've been meaning to do for your teenager but never seem to have the time (or energy or motivation) to tackle? Something that gets grandfathered onto every mental to-do list but never gets crossed off? Something your teen has likely given up hope of ever seeing completed? Finishing that task would be a great way of announcing your intention to learn your teen's love language. What steps do you need to take this week to complete that task?

STEP 1

STEP 2

STEP 3

STEP 4

STEP 5

STEP 6

Use this space for more notes, quotes, or lessons learned from the chapter.

OBJECTIVE

In reading this chapter, you will learn how to use well-chosen gifts
to express love in ways that fill your teenager's emotional love tank.

LOVE LANGUAGE #5: GIFTS

INSTRUCTIONS: Complete this seventh lesson after reading chapter 7 ("Love Language #5: Gifts," pp. 127–144) of *The 5 Love Languages of Teenagers*.

KEY TERM

Gifts: a love language in which a person experiences emotional wholeness through well-chosen presents.

OPENING QUESTIONS

1. What's the best gift anyone could ever give you? Let your imagination run wild. Maybe your ideal gift would be to spend one more day with a loved one who passed away. Or to see your favorite team win a championship. Why would that gift resonate so powerfully with you? What's the closest approximation of that gift you can think of? For example, a photo collage of your deceased loved one or a video clip of the two of you together.

2. If you asked the same question of your teenager, what are some gifts he or she might name? Why would those gifts be especially meaningful for your teen? What's the closest approximation of those gifts you can think of?

THINK ABOUT IT

3. Dr. Chapman warns, **"For some parents, almost all of what they call 'gifts' are in fact efforts at manipulating their teenager, bartering for something they desire, or payment for the teenager's work."** Give an example of a "gift" that involves manipulation, bartering, or payment. What question must a parent ask to determine whether a gift is genuine?

4. What is the ultimate purpose of gift-giving? What do givers want recipients to sense deeply from their gifts? What happens when parents diminish the ceremony of gift-giving? How can parents make gift-giving a strong vehicle of emotional love?

5. Dr. Chapman points out, **"Sincere parents often ask, 'If I give too many gifts to my teenagers, won't I foster the spirit of materialism that is so prevalent in our culture?'"** What other questions are parents wise to ask? According to Dr. Chapman, **"materialism is a poor substitute for"** what?

6. Regarding giving money as a gift, Dr. Chapman says, **"One might think that if giving gifts is one of the primary love languages, and if parents are giving all this money to their teenagers, then the teenager's love tank should be full."** What two problems with this reasoning does he identify? What two approaches does he recommend for giving money?

7. Give an example of when you would need to consider your teen's welfare before you give him or her a specific gift. Give an example of how you would consider your teenager's interests before you give him or her a specific gift.

8. Dr. Chapman shared the story of giving his daughter a golden key on a golden chain as a private gift from him to her. What might a private gift from you to your teen look like? In addition to private gifts, Dr. Chapman emphasizes the importance of treasured gifts, which **"become symbols of love in the heart of the teenager for years to come."** What might a treasured gift from you to your teen look like?

9. What are counterfeit gifts? Why are they given? Why are they unlikely to fill a teenager's emotional love tank?

TAKE IT HOME

If your teenager's primary love language is gifts, you need to understand that not every gift you give will fill his or her emotional love tank. Remember, the way you present your gift is every bit as important—if not more so—as what you give. For native speakers of the gifts love language, it truly is the thought that counts. For each of the following gift-giving scenarios, write down some ideas for making the gift more meaningful.

Brady needs a new pair of running shoes. Before a Saturday cross-country practice, his dad takes him to Runners World and buys him an expensive pair of running shoes. Brady wears the shoes to practice, and that's the last time he gives much thought to them.

Amy picked out the dress she wants for prom. Her mom agrees to buy it for her if Amy will drive her brothers to and from their fast-food jobs for the next two weeks.

After getting a bonus at work, Matt's father decides to give Matt a cash gift of $500.

A GIFT A DAY

On the calendar below, plan a special week of gift-giving. Think of something special you can give your teenager each day. You don't have to overextend your budget. Remember, gifts don't have to be expensive to be meaningful. But all seven should be meaningful. You might also write down some creative ideas as to where and how you might give each gift.

SUNDAY	
MONDAY	
TUESDAY	
WEDNESDAY	
THURSDAY	
FRIDAY	
SATURDAY	

LOVE CHALLENGE

In question 2 of this lesson, you imagined the ideal gift for your teenager and the closest approximation of it that you could think of. What steps will you take this week to make that approximation happen and prepare to give your teen a memorable gift?

STEP 1

STEP 2

STEP 3

STEP 4

STEP 5

STEP 6

Use this space for more notes, quotes, or lessons learned from the chapter.

OBJECTIVE

In reading this chapter, you will learn how to confirm your teenager's primary love language—and perhaps discover new dialects and a secondary love language—so that you can work smarter in making your teen feel truly loved.

DISCOVER YOUR TEENAGER'S PRIMARY LOVE LANGUAGE

INSTRUCTIONS: Complete this eighth lesson after reading chapter 8 ("Discover Your Teenager's Primary Love Language," pp. 147–164) of *The 5 Love Languages of Teenagers*.

KEY TERM

Disequilibrium: emotional instability caused by the rapidly changing thoughts, feelings, and desires teenagers experience.

OPENING QUESTIONS

1. What are the biggest changes you notice in your child since he or she entered the teenage years? How do you react to those changes? In what ways have those changes affected your relationship with your teen?

2. In what areas do you still see traces of the child your teenager used to be? Describe the challenge of nurturing your teenager during the difficult transition to adulthood while still wanting to hang on to those traces of childhood.

THINK ABOUT IT

3. Dr. Chapman describes three specific challenges that parents face in trying to speak their teenager's primary love language. What does teenage moodiness look like in your home? How does it affect your efforts to speak your teen's primary love language? What does the teenage quest for independence look like in your home? How does it affect your efforts to speak your teen's primary love language? What does teenage anger—or a withdrawn attitude—look like in your home? How does it affect your efforts to speak your teen's primary love language?

4. Dr. Chapman assures parents that their child's primary love language didn't change when he or she became a teenager. What are three reasons parents might assume that it did?

5. What is Dr. Chapman's advice to the parent who says, **"I'm doing the same thing I did when he was a child but now he is not responding"**? What might learning a new dialect look like with your child?

6. Dr. Chapman writes, **"You have to ask questions if you want to know what is going on inside your teenager's head."** Why is that often easier said than done? How would you phrase a question to discover more about your teenager's primary love language?

7. Dr. Chapman recommends, **"Consciously observe the behavior of your teenager."** What three areas should a parent focus on? What will those three areas reveal about your teen?

8. Describe the five-week experiment involving all five love languages that Dr. Chapman recommends for discovering your teen's primary love language. What might the second experiment, involving giving your teen two choices, look like in your home? Once you discover your teenager's primary love language, why is it important to learn as many different dialects as possible?

9. Why is your learning to speak all five love languages important to your teenager's future relationships? How will it also benefit your marriage?

TAKE IT HOME

Dr. Chapman writes, **"If this book is your first exposure to the concept of the love languages—you didn't look for [your teen's] primary love language when he was a child—and you haven't a clue about how to figure out his primary love language now that he's a teenager, let me suggest three steps. First, you've got to ask questions; then make some observations; and third, experiment."**

What questions would work best in getting your teen to talk about what makes him or her feel loved?

How does your teen express love to you and others?

What patterns do you see in your teen's most frequent requests and complaints?

Try different types of physical touch with your teen, everything from hugs to high fives to playful wrestling matches. How does your teen respond to your physical touch?

Offer frequent words of affirmation to your teen. Focus on several different aspects of his or her personality and behavior. How does your teen respond to your words of affirmation?

Set aside blocks of uninterrupted time to spend with your teen. This might involve anything from going shopping together to kicking a soccer ball around. How does your teen respond to spending quality time with you?

Give your teen a few gifts that appeal to his or her specific interests—anything from an item they collect to a new fish for their aquarium. How does your teen respond to the gifts?

Perform a few acts of service for your teen—anything from redecorating his or her room to creating a study guide for a midterm exam. How does your teen respond to your acts of service?

A GAME PLAN FOR THE TEENAGE YEARS

I believe my teen's primary love language is _____.

Here's why I think so:

When my child was younger, I spoke his or her love language by . . .

Since my child became a teenager, I've started to notice that he or she . . .

I think my teen might respond well to a different dialect—that is, a different way of speaking his or her love language. One dialect I'm going to try is . . .

I'm also going to explore the possibility that my teen speaks a secondary love language. Here's what I'm going to do to discover it:

To make sure that my teen's emotional love tank stays full, I'm going to . . .

LOVE CHALLENGE

What steps will you take this week to reevaluate your teenager's primary love language? What dialects—or different ways of speaking that love language—will you start to experiment with? What steps will you take to see if your teen has a secondary love language?

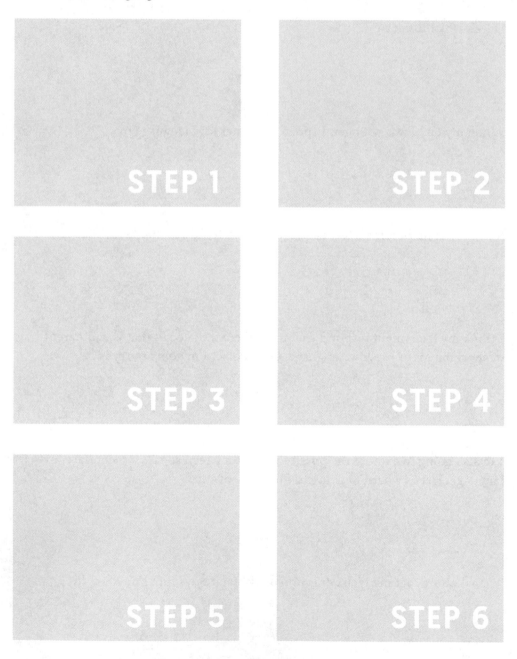

STEP 1

STEP 2

STEP 3

STEP 4

STEP 5

STEP 6

Use this space for more notes, quotes, or lessons learned from the chapter.

OBJECTIVE

In reading this chapter, you will learn how to process and express your anger in a way that's healthy to you and your family so that you can, in turn, help your teenager learn to process and express anger in a healthy way.

ANGER AND TEENAGERS

INSTRUCTIONS: Complete this ninth lesson after reading chapter 9 ("Anger and Teenagers," pp. 167–191) of *The 5 Love Languages of Teenagers.*

KEY
TERM

Mismanaged anger: anger that is expressed in unhealthy ways, causing emotional damage and creating obstacles in the parent-teen relationship.

OPENING QUESTIONS

1. Name three things that cause you to see red in an instant. They don't necessarily have to be justifiable, or even reasonable, causes—just three things that trigger immediate anger in you.

2. How do you usually express anger? Do you see that as healthy or unhealthy? Explain. How does your teenager express anger? Do you see that as healthy or unhealthy? Explain.

THINK ABOUT IT

3. Dr. Chapman points out, **"The teen's increased intellectual abilities to reason and think critically about issues allow him to question our judgment in a way he did not do as a child."** How do these increased abilities often put a teenager in conflict with his or her parents? What response does that trigger in a parent? Why is it essential for parents to take the initiative in dealing with their misplaced anger?

4. What are the four steps Dr. Chapman suggests for breaking destructive patterns and establishing loving patterns of anger management? What would be an effective strategy for you to break destructive anger patterns? If you believe your anger is valid, how would you communicate that to the loved one who triggered it?

5. Dr. Chapman writes, **"Most teenagers lean toward one of these destructive approaches to anger: implosion or explosion."** What are the differences between the two? Which approach does your teenager usually take? How do you react to your teenager's approach to anger?

6. Why is listening to your teenager's expressions of anger—no matter how harshly they are delivered—so important? Why does Dr. Chapman say parents should be thankful when their teenager expresses anger verbally? What happens when parents get angry at the way their teen is talking to them? What hard questions do parents of silent teens need to ask?

7. How does Dr. Chapman answer the parent who asks, **"How can I affirm [my teenager's] anger when I don't agree with their perception?"** Why is empathy essential in affirming your teenager's emotions? What does empathy involve for a parent?

8. What happens if parents try to explain their perspective and seek resolution before they listen to their teen and affirm that his or her angry feelings are valid? What should parents do if, after listening to their teen's perspective, they realize that their teen is right? What should they do if they disagree with their teen's perspective?

9. Dr. Chapman closes the chapter by sharing a powerful poem he received from his son. What would you like for your teen to write about you someday? Explain.

TAKE IT HOME

Dr. Chapman says the first step in **"breaking destructive patterns and establishing loving patterns of anger management"** is to **"admit the truth."** Here's your chance to do so. In the space below, write your admission of how you've mismanaged your anger in the past. Talk about how you plan to change. Include a strategy for what you want your family to do if you fall back into your old habits.

After you share your admission with your family, tear out this page and keep it where you can see it often—ideally, next to a picture of your teen. Let it serve as a reminder of what you're working for.

FOSTERING POSITIVE ANGER MANAGEMENT SKILLS

Dr Chapman writes, **"I suggest to parents that you observe your teenager when he is angry and keep a record of how he processes his anger toward you or toward others. Two months of observation will show you where your teenager is in the development of positive anger management skills."** Use this sheet as needed to guide your observation process.

Is your teenager's response to anger usually implosive or explosive?

What happens when your teen gets angry?

What words, if any, does your teen use when he or she gets angry?

What statement or question will you use to invite your teen to clarify what you heard them say?

If your teen chooses silence as a response to anger, what hard questions will you ask yourself?

What message or confession will you communicate to your silent teen?

LOVE CHALLENGE

On the "Take It Home" page, you admitted to past incidents of unhealthy or destructive anger management. What steps will you take this week to share your admission with your family and enlist their efforts to help you change?

STEP 1

STEP 2

STEP 3

STEP 4

STEP 5

STEP 6

Use this space for more notes, quotes, or lessons learned from the chapter.

OBJECTIVE

In reading this chapter, you will learn how to recognize the unique
emotional needs of a teenager in a single-parent or blended family
and keep his or her emotional love tank filled.

LOVING YOUR TEEN IN SINGLE-PARENT AND BLENDED FAMILIES

INSTRUCTIONS: Complete this tenth lesson after reading chapter 10 ("Loving Your Teen in Single-Parent and Blended Families," pp. 193–223) of *The 5 Love Languages of Teenagers*.

KEY TERM

Disneyland Daddy: a noncustodial parent who spends his time with his teenager focusing on activities rather than on the teenager.

OPENING QUESTIONS

1. Name three challenges of being a single parent that married parents don't face.

2. Name three challenges of raising a teenager in a blended family that parents in non-blended families don't face.

THINK ABOUT IT

3. Dr. Chapman recalls his conversation with Amanda, a single parent who admitted, **"I'm not sure I'm up to this. I think I've done fairly well up until now, but I don't know if I can endure the teenage years."** How prepared are you to handle your child's teenage years? Explain. What do you see as the most difficult challenges that lie ahead?

4. Dr. Chapman writes, **"Feelings buried in childhood often erupt in the teenage years."** How do the emotions of hurt, anger, and rejection that were seldom expressed in childhood make themselves known in the teenage years? How are these strong emotions connected to your teen's developing desire for independence and self-identity?

5. Why is it important for parents to focus on their teenager's emotions rather than their behavior? What happens when teens are encouraged to express hurtful emotions from the past instead of being condemned for their negative behavior?

6. Dr. Chapman illustrates the challenges that custodial parents face by pointing out their tendency to give simple, vague answers to their child's questions about their noncustodial parent and the breakup of the relationship. What happens when the child becomes a teenager? What specific questions might your teenager ask?

7. Why is the "Disneyland Daddy" approach to parenting ultimately unfulfilling for teenagers? How can a noncustodial parent involve his or her teen in the normal flow of life without taking advantage of the teen's time or willingness to help? Why are teens often reluctant to share their emotional struggles with their noncustodial parent? How can a wise noncustodial parent create an atmosphere that encourages such sharing?

8. What are the six guidelines that Dr. Chapman recommends to both custodial and noncustodial parents for showing love to their teenagers? Which one presents the biggest challenge to you? Explain. What will you need to do to rise to that challenge?

9. Dr. Chapman points out, **"Most teenagers find life in the blended family extremely difficult."** What factors make it so difficult? What happens if the teenager's resentment isn't processed in a healthy way? Why are teenagers often slow in responding to the love of a stepparent? What can a stepparent do to overcome these barriers?

TAKE IT HOME

Dr. Chapman writes that one statement he hears frequently from single parents is **"Will someone please help me? I'm not sure I can do this by myself."** Nor should anyone have to. If you're a single parent, you need a team of people who care about you and your child—a support group you trust. No one can assemble that team for you because you have the final say on who you will allow to influence your child. Listed below, you'll find some possibilities to consider. (Add your own ideas in the blank spaces.) On a scale of one to ten, rate how feasible or advisable it would be to enlist each for your support team. Write a brief explanation for each rating, along with any ideas for making that person a more feasible helper.

PERSON	RATING	COMMENT
Parent(s)		
Sibling(s)		
Grandparent(s)		
Aunt(s)/Uncle(s)/ Cousin(s)		
Friend(s)		
Coworker(s)		
Neighbor(s)		
Pastor/Spiritual Leader(s)		
Your Ex-in-Law(s)		

CHALLENGES AND RESPONSES

Obviously, there's no way to predict every challenge you'll face in a single-parent or blended family. But you can prepare for some of the most common ones. Using Dr. Chapman's advice, how would you respond to the following situations?

CHALLENGE	RESPONSE
Your teenager begins to criticize your parenting skills.	
Your teenager needs quality time with you, but between work, school, and household responsibilities, quality time is hard to come by.	
Finding privacy in our home is nearly impossible, and leaving the house isn't always an option.	
Your teenager starts asking hard questions about your ex— and the answers may hurt your teen.	
Your teenager chafes at his or her stepparent's new rules.	

LOVE CHALLENGE

Dr. Chapman says to single parents, **"You need not walk alone; there are people in your community who care. Keep searching until you find them."** If you're a single parent, what can you do this week to meet your own need for love and companionship? What would make a difference in your life right now? Who can you reach out to for company and conversation? If you're not a single parent, but you know one, what can you do this week to show love and companionship to that person?

Use this space for more notes, quotes, or lessons learned from the chapter.

OBJECTIVE

In reading this chapter, you will learn how to accommodate your teenager's desire for independence while providing the love and guidance he or she needs.

LOVE AND THE DESIRE FOR INDEPENDENCE

INSTRUCTIONS: Complete this eleventh lesson after reading chapter 11 ("Love and the Desire for Independence," pp. 225–245) of *The 5 Love Languages of Teenagers.*

KEY TERM

Emotional independence: the freedom to share, or not share, one's thoughts, feelings, and experiences.

OPENING QUESTIONS

1. What were some of your early milestones in your quest for independence? What did each one mean to you? What were some of your stumbles along the way? What did you learn from them?

2. What is your number one concern when it comes to your teenager's quest for independence? What would your teen say about that concern?

THINK ABOUT IT

3. Dr. Chapman begins the chapter by describing his consultation with Matt and Lori, parents who were blindsided by their son's "suddenly" becoming a teenager. Dr. Chapman summarizes their fear and confusion this way: **"Everything changes so fast—seemingly overnight. What worked before suddenly no longer works, and the child they thought they knew so well has suddenly become a stranger."** Which parts of his summary ring true for you? How would you describe your child's teenage transition?

4. During which two periods do parents often have heightened conflict with their children? What common thread ties these periods together? What should be the parents' goal during their child's teenage years?

5. Dr. Chapman points out, **"The teenager wants to be a part of the family but at the same time wants to be independent from the family."** What are your guidelines for giving your child personal space in a public setting? What are your guidelines for giving your child personal space in your home? What are your guidelines for giving your child the freedom that a car offers?

6. Dr. Chapman writes, **"One way teenagers establish emotional independence is by keeping their thoughts and feelings to themselves."** How do wise parents respond to being "shut out" by their teen? How do wise parents respond when their teen's desire for emotional independence involves pulling away from expressions of love he or she used to receive?

7. Dr. Chapman reminds parents that their teen's desire for social independence—the desire to be with friends—is not a rejection of parents; instead, **"it is evidence that his social horizons are widening beyond the family."** How can you encourage social independence in your teenager?

8. If you wish to be an influential part of your teenager's reasoning process, what must you do? What might that sound like in your relationship with your teen? What is the best way to respond if your teenager's quest for intellectual independence involves questioning your religious beliefs?

9. What happens if parents recognize their teen's right to make independent decisions and are willing to invest the time and create the atmosphere for meaningful dialogue in a loving setting? What happens if parents draw lines in the sand and make dogmatic statements about what their teen is going to believe and do?

TAKE IT HOME

Though there are some common elements in the teenage quest for independence, every teen's pursuit is unique. For each of the following scenarios, write the unique challenges you face with your teen. For example, your teen may already have his or her own room but may be pressing to redecorate it so that it's not so childish.

YOUR TEEN'S DESIRE FOR PERSONAL SPACE IN PUBLIC

Think about how your teen acts at church or the store or a restaurant or a school event or any other place where he or she might be seen with you.

YOUR TEEN'S DESIRE FOR PERSONAL SPACE AT HOME

Think about how your teen expresses a need for privacy and tries to create his or her own niche in your house.

YOUR TEEN'S DESIRE FOR INDEPENDENT TRANSPORTATION

Think about how your teen expresses a need for a car.

YOUR TEEN'S DESIRE FOR EMOTIONAL SPACE

Think about how your teen chooses what, when, and with whom to share the details of his or her life.

YOUR TEEN'S DESIRE FOR SOCIAL INDEPENDENCE

Think about how your teen expresses the desire to spend time with friends instead of family, listen to the music he or she likes, and dress the way he or she chooses.

YOUR TEEN'S DESIRE FOR INTELLECTUAL INDEPENDENCE

Think about how your teen's attitude has changed when it comes to values, morals, or religious beliefs.

ANTICIPATING CRITICAL MOMENTS

If your goal is to help your teen make a smooth transition from dependence to independence, you need to be prepared to say the right thing at critical moments. Here are a few things your teen may say that bring on those critical moments. With Dr. Chapman's advice in mind, write your best response to each one.

YOUR TEENAGER SAYS . . .	YOU SAY . . .
"I can't do family movie night on Friday. Tyler and his parents invited me to go out on their boat with them."	
"I want to put a deadbolt lock on my bedroom door so that no one can come in without my permission."	
"I need my own car. You don't realize how embarrassing it is to be driven everywhere by your parents."	

LOVE CHALLENGE

What is the most pressing need for independence in your teenager's life right now? What steps will you take this week to give your teen more independence in that area?

STEP 1

STEP 2

STEP 3

STEP 4

STEP 5

STEP 6

Use this space for more notes, quotes, or lessons learned from the chapter.

OBJECTIVE

In reading this chapter, you will learn how to help your teenager
appreciate the importance of boundaries and involve him or her
in the process of setting fair and effective household rules.

LOVE AND THE NEED FOR RESPONSIBILITY

INSTRUCTIONS: Complete this twelfth lesson after reading chapter 12 ("Love and the Need for Responsibility," pp. 247–268) of *The 5 Love Languages of Teenagers*.

KEY TERM

Dictatorial: an unloving approach to rule-making that favors the arbitrary use of power, with little explanation of the rules, and no outside input on their formation.

OPENING QUESTIONS

1. On a scale of one to ten, with one being "Anarchist" and ten being "Complete Conformist," how much of a rule follower were you when you were a teenager? How do you explain your attitude toward rules back in the day? How does it affect your attitude toward the household rules you set for your teenager?

2. How many rules do you have in your household? Would you say you have too many, too few, or just the right number? How would your teenager answer that question? If your teenager could get rid of one rule, what would it be?

THINK ABOUT IT

3. According to Dr. Chapman, what is independence without responsibility? How will you explain the connection between the two to your teenager?

4. True or false? Teenagers will rebel if parents establish boundaries. Explain. What is it that causes teens to rebel? Why doesn't "Because I said so" work with teenagers?

5. Dr. Chapman says, **"Wise parents will bring their teenagers into the circle of decision-making—letting them express their ideas on what constitutes fair and/or worthy rules."** What happens when a teenager has a voice in making a rule? What would a family decision-making forum look like in your home? What principle should guide your teen's involvement in making household rules?

6. What happens when a teenager striving for independence feels loved by his or her parents? On the other hand, what happens when a teenager striving for independence doesn't feel loved by his or her parents? What strategy does Dr. Chapman recommend for rethinking and reforming childish household rules?

7. What are three guidelines for rule-making that make the process manageable and purposeful? What are the really important issues you want to focus on with your household rules? How can you make each one as clear as possible? Why is fairness so important in the rule-making process?

8. Dr. Chapman says, **"Rules without consequences are not only worthless, but they are also confusing."** How do consequences foster responsible living? What are some examples from daily life that illustrate that point? What three guidelines should parents keep in mind when they formulate and enforce consequences?

9. What two questions should guide your thinking when it comes to establishing areas of responsibility for your teenager? What six common areas does Dr. Chapman identify as needing rules and consequences? Of the six, which area presents the biggest challenge for you? Explain. What steps can you take to meet that challenge head-on and establish rules and consequences that will help your teen become more independent and more responsible?

TAKE IT HOME

Dr. Chapman writes, **"If this process of teenage independence and responsibility is to move smoothly, parents must help it along with the right language of love."** One challenge parents face is figuring out how to show love to their teen while upholding household rules that he or she chafes at. The key to rising to this challenge is empathy—understanding your teen's perspective, feeling what he or she is feeling. Here's a chance for you to practice. Think of a household rule that causes friction with your teen and fill in the following information.

The rule, as stated in our family:

The reason the rule is in place:

I believe the rule is fair because . . .

My teen would like to see the rule changed because . . .

I can empathize with my teen because . . .

I can show my empathy by . . .

FORMING RULES WITH YOUR TEENAGER

Dr. Chapman says, **"Wise parents will bring their teenagers into the circle of decision-making—letting them express their ideas on what constitutes fair and/or worthy rules."** Below you'll find the keys areas Dr. Chapman mentions in which household rules are needed. For each area, write your preferred rules, your teen's preferred rules, and ways (if any) you can compromise.

"AROUND THE HOUSE" RESPONSIBILITES		
Your Preferred Rules	*Your Teen's Preferred Rules*	*Compromise*

SCHOOLWORK		
Your Preferred Rules	*Your Teen's Preferred Rules*	*Compromise*

USE OF AUTOMOBILES		
Your Preferred Rules	*Your Teen's Preferred Rules*	*Compromise*

MONEY MANAGEMENT		
Your Preferred Rules	*Your Teen's Preferred Rules*	*Compromise*

DATING		
Your Preferred Rules	*Your Teen's Preferred Rules*	*Compromise*

ALCOHOL AND DRUGS		
Your Preferred Rules	*Your Teen's Preferred Rules*	*Compromise*

LOVE CHALLENGE

What steps will you take this week to bring your teenager into your family's "circle of decision-making"? Which rules will you focus on first?

Use this space for more notes, quotes, or lessons learned from the chapter.

OBJECTIVE

In reading this chapter, you will learn how to show your teenager
the necessary love and guidance to overcome a personal failure.

LOVING WHEN YOUR TEEN FAILS

INSTRUCTIONS: Complete this thirteenth lesson after reading chapter 13 ("Loving When Your Teen Fails," pp. 271–287) of *The 5 Love Languages of Teenagers.*

KEY TERM

Moral failure: the violation of a moral code by which a family has lived through the years.

OPENING QUESTIONS

1. If you could change one mistake—one past failure in your life—what would it be? Why? How did you parents respond to your failure? What, if anything, do you wish they had done differently?

2. If you asked your teenager those same questions, what do you think he or she would say?

THINK ABOUT IT

3. Dr. Chapman reminds us, **"Teenagers are their own people, and they are free to make choices: good and bad."** Why do parents suffer when their teen makes poor choices?

4. Describe a time when your teenager failed to meet your performance expectations. How did you react? What, if anything, do you regret about your reaction? What factors must parents consider when it comes to performance "failures"?

5. In what two ways do teenagers violate moral codes? Describe a teenage moral failure that you're aware of—if not in your own family, then in that of someone you know well. How did the parents react? What impact did the failure have on the family?

6. What practical ideas does Dr. Chapman offer for processing teenage moral failure in a redemptive manner? Why is it counterproductive for parents to blame themselves for the failure? Why is it counterproductive for parents to "preach"? Why is it counterproductive for parents to try to fix the problem?

7. Why is unconditional love essential for a teenager who's failed in a moral sense? What kind of support should parents offer? What types of guidance should parents offer?

8. What is the best thing parents can do to prevent teenage failure through alcohol and drugs? What specific preventative measures can you take to make sure that your teen is aware of the real-life consequences of alcohol and drug use? What steps can you take if your teen is past the preventative stage?

9. Daniel and Micki, two parents who were devastated to learn of their son's moral failure, were later able to say, **"The darkest night of our lives was the beginning of a deeper and more meaningful relationship with our teenager."** What is the key for turning tragedy into triumph? What does a teen who has experienced failure need from his or her parents?

TAKE IT HOME

To help your teen develop a healthy perspective toward failure, try helping him or her put different types of failure in perspective so that he or she understands their implications. For each of the following categories, list three or four that your teen might experience. For example, a minor failure is one that may sting temporarily but will likely be forgotten in a day or two. A bad test grade might be considered a minor failure. A serious failure is one that may have some lingering implications. Causing an automobile accident because of distracted driving might qualify as a serious failure. A life changer is self-explanatory: a failure whose repercussions alter life as you know it.

MINOR FAILURES	SERIOUS FAILURES	LIFE CHANGERS

WORKING THROUGH A MORAL FAILURE

Moral failures come in all shapes and sizes, but there's one thing they all have in common: survivability. You can help your teen work through a moral failure by following the seven steps Dr. Chapman identifies. Here's a chance for you to practice. Imagine that your teen confesses a moral failure to you.

How would you take responsibility for your own parenting choices without blaming yourself for your teen's failure?

What would you say to your teen instead of preaching to him or her?

How could you "fix" the situation? How would you resist the urge to try?

How could you show your teen unconditional love in this situation?

How could you help your teen understand that you empathize?

How could you show your teen tangible support?

What guidance would you offer your teen?

LOVE CHALLENGE

If you're like most parents, you probably regret at least one or two past responses to failure in your child's life. You can send a signal to your teen that you're serious about taking a different approach by apologizing for those past responses and asking for forgiveness. What steps will you take this week to make amends for those past responses?

STEP 1

STEP 2

STEP 3

STEP 4

STEP 5

STEP 6

Use this space for more notes, quotes, or lessons learned from the chapter.

THE 5 LOVE LANGUAGES OF TEENAGERS LEADER'S GUIDE

Congratulations! You're on the cusp of an exciting adventure. You're about to lead a small group through thirteen studies that will enrich relationships and change lives. And you'll have a front-row seat to it all.

You'll find that every small group presents its own unique challenges and opportunities. But there are some tips that can help you get the most out of any small-group study, whether you're a seasoned veteran or a first-time leader.

1. Communicate.

From the outset, you'll want to give members a sense of how your group dynamic will work. To maximize your time together, group members will need to read each lesson's assigned chapter of *The 5 Love Languages of Teenagers* and then complete the "Opening Questions" (questions 1–2) and "Think About It" section (questions 3–9) *before* the meeting. The "Take It Home" and "Love Challenge" activities should be completed after the meeting.

2. Keep a good pace.

Your first meeting will begin with introductions (if necessary). After that, you'll ask group members to share their responses to the first two "Getting Started" questions. These are icebreakers. Their purpose is merely to introduce the session topic. You'll want to give everyone a chance to share, but you don't want to get sidetracked by overly long discussions here.

The "Think About It" section (questions 3–9) is the heart of the study. This is where most of your discussion should occur. You'll need to establish a good pace, making sure that you give each question its due while allowing enough time to tackle all of them. After you've finished your discussion of the questions, briefly go over the "Take It Home" and "Love Challenge" sections, so that group members know what their "homework" will be.

Your next meeting will begin with a brief review of that homework. Ask volunteers to share their responses to the "Take It Home" activities and their experiences in implementing the "Love Challenge." After about five minutes of reviewing your group members' application of the previous lesson, begin your new lesson.

3. Prepare.

Read each chapter, answer the study questions, and work through the take-home material, just like your group members will do. Try to anticipate questions or comments your group members will have. If you have time, think of stories from your own parenting experience or from the experiences of people you know that apply to the lesson. That way, if you have a lull during your study, you can use the stories to spark conversation.

4. Be open and vulnerable.

Not everyone is comfortable with sharing the details of their parenting experience with other people. Yet openness and vulnerability are essential in a group setting. That's where you come in. If you have the courage to be vulnerable, to share less-than-flattering details about your own experience, you may give others the courage to do the same.

5. Emphasize and celebrate the uniqueness of every parent.

Some group members may feel intimidated by other people's seemingly successful parenting. Others may find that strategies for learning love languages that work for some people don't work for them—and they may get discouraged. You can head off that discouragement by opening up about your own struggles and successes. Help group members see that, beneath the surface, every parent faces challenges.

6. Create a safe haven where people feel free—and comfortable—to share.

Ask group members to agree to some guidelines before your first meeting. For example, what is said in the group setting stays in the group setting. And every person's voice deserves to be heard. If you find that some group members are quick to give unsolicited advice or criticism when other people share, remind the group that every parenting situation is unique. What works for one may not work for another. If the problem persists, talk with your advice givers and critics one-on-one. Help them see how their well-intended comments may be having the unintended effect of discouraging others from talking.

7. Follow up.

The questions and activities in this book encourage group members to incorporate new strategies with their children and make significant changes to their parenting routines. You can be the cheerleader your group members need by celebrating their successes and congratulating them for their courage and commitment. Also, by checking in each week with your group members, you create accountability and give them motivation to apply *The 5 Love Languages of Teenagers* principles to their relationships.

THE SECRET TO GREAT RELATIONSHIPS—JUST FOR TEENS

Simple ways to
strengthen relationships.

- TAKE THE LOVE LANGUAGE® QUIZ

- DOWNLOAD FREE RESOURCES AND STUDY GUIDES

- BROWSE THE LOVE LANGUAGE® GIFT GUIDE

- SUBSCRIBE TO PODCASTS

- SHOP THE STORE

- SIGN UP FOR THE NEWSLETTER

Visit www.5lovelanguages.com

HAS TECHNOLOGY TAKEN OVER YOUR HOME?

Take back your family and home from the overwhelming presence of technology.

Also available as an eBook and audiobook

BREAK YOUR FAMILY FREE FROM TECHNOLOGY'S TRANCE

Get the tips and tools you and your family need to avoid the pitfalls of today's screen-based technology, while still enjoying its benefits.

Available for purchase at
5lovelanguages.com/store/winning-the-screen-wars

CONNECT WITH YOUR FAMILY WITHOUT BREAKING THE BANK.

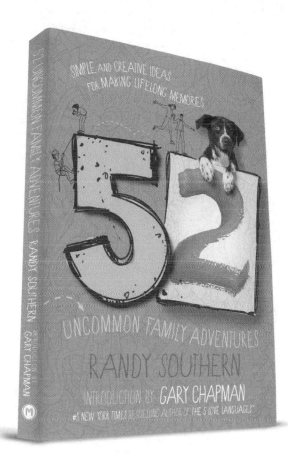

Whether it's a family pillow fight, a lip-sync competition, or Toilet Paper Olympics, give your family the gift of lifelong memories while having fun, connecting spiritually, and speaking each other's love languages. Enjoy all the benefits of the quality time you dreamed of without all the pressure of advanced planning.

Also available as an eBook